# Prayerful Plea

A 30-Day Prayer Devotional

Shirley J. Johnson

Still Joyful Ministries

Publisher: Still Joyful Ministries

Cover Design: Shirley J. Johnson

Printed in the United States of America

ISBN Print: 978-1-7332787-3-7

ISBN eBook: 978-1-7332787-4-4

# Contents

# Acknowledgements

**Father, Son, Holy Spirit**

God shaped me, Jesus saved me, and the Holy Spirit speaks to me. Without the Holy Trinity, I would be a lost soul without direction. Thank you, Lord, for changing me, restoring me, sustaining me and growing me into my purpose. Thank You for teaching me how to intercede for myself and for others. I am forever grateful.

**To My Husband, Tremaine M. Johnson**

I wouldn't give you a chance to talk to me when we first met, but now I have the absolute best conversations with you. You love me from a place that does not judge or look at me through a flawed lens. You support me better, bolder, and safer than anyone else. You pray for me, you protect me, and you love me as Christ loved the church. You are the one who allows me to be me with no hidden motives or agendas. I love you for loving me as I am. Ditto (you know).

**Lisa Bell DBA Radical Women**

You are the absolute best, and I cannot ever imagine writing anything without you as a part of the process. You are faith-filled, patient, caring, and you allow writers to have their own voice. You are a real example of God's love on Earth. Thank you simply for being you and for being willing to work with me. You will never know just how much you have blessed me.

# Key Terms

**Prayer:**
1. a devout petition to God or an object of worship.
2. a spiritual communion with God or an object of worship, as in supplication, thanksgiving, adoration, or confession.

**Intercession:**
2. an interposing or pleading on behalf of another person.
3. a prayer to God on behalf of another.

**Plea:**
1. an appeal or entreaty

**Supplication:**
1. an act or instance of supplicating; humble prayer, entreaty, or petition.

**Worship:**
1. reverent honor and homage paid to God or a sacred personage, or to any object regarded as sacred.

**Adoration:**
1. the act of paying honor, as to a divine being; worship.

2. reverent homage.

**Repentance:**
1. deep sorrow, compunction, or contrition for a past sin, wrongdoing, or the like.

# Prayer Preparation

*You don't have to be profound with God, but you do need to be proactive in your prayer life.*

SJJ

**Choose a place that is quiet.**

- Although not required, it helps to utilize the same space (closet, office, room, porch, etc.) It creates a familiar space for you and allows for a saturated atmosphere of continual prayer—meeting place.

**Keep your prayer tools close by.**

- Bible (Studying the Bible often assists with hearing in prayer. It also strengthens your walk and maturity.)

- Pen, pencil, and highlighter.

- Paper, journal, index cards, prayer cards.

- A prayer board or prayer container works great.

**Note:** *I like to put prayer requests up on my prayer board so I can see them daily. It is a daily reminder to cover others. I place them into a container after God has answered the prayers.*

## Set the atmosphere.

- Peace and quiet is best.

- Water sounds, soaking music, or instrumentals are very helpful if you are easily distracted or sit still better with background noise. Hearing music with words will often deter your focus and ability to hear clearly.

## Eliminate distractions.

- Silence/turn off your phone.

- Silence alarms.

- If you have children or a spouse, assure this is a time you do not need to give attention to them.

## Invite the Holy Spirit to commune with you.

- The Holy Spirit is your comforter and will guide you.

Ask the Lord Jesus what is on His heart and how you should pray.

- The Father (God), The Son (Jesus), and the Holy Spirit/Holy Ghost are with you.

- Quiet your mind.

*Note: Focus on prayer and immediately quiet any distractions that try to enter your mind. At this time, nothing and no one are more important than your time with the Lord in prayer.*

* Listen more than you talk. It is helpful to develop a listening ear as well as a praying tongue. Many of us go into prayer asking for His blessings versus seeking out His will.

## Do not set a time limit.

* Do not set a time limit for prayer unless you absolutely have to. Prayer is not about the length of time you pray. It is about the sincerity of your prayers and connection with the One who listens, responds, and answers your plea.

*Note: The instructions above are for your quiet time with the Lord. Please know that prayer can be accomplished anywhere and in any atmosphere. Pray whenever you need to call on the Lord. Prayer is not place-driven. Places do not limit the power of prayer nor hinder your ability to call out to the Lord in prayer. When you think of prayer, imagine a lifeline you cannot allow to flatline. You are the pulse, and God is the giver of your rhythm. Stay in tune with Him and stay in continual prayer.*

# Prayer Points

U se these scriptures to become familiar with prayer in the Bible. Some days you may not have time to pray and journal your thoughts, but there is always time for a scripture. Use one of these scriptures to meditate on and try to memorize it. This will help with hiding the Word in your heart.

**Job 42:10**
And the Lord restored Job's losses when he prayed for his friends. Indeed, the Lord gave Job twice as much as he had before.

**Psalm 5:3**
"My voice You shall hear in the morning, O Lord; In the morning, I will direct it to You, and I will look up."

**Psalm 19:14**
"Let the words of my mouth and the meditation of my heart be acceptable in Your sight, O Lord, my strength and my Redeemer."

**Psalm 39:12**
"Hear my prayer, O Lord, and give ear to my cry; do not be silent at my tears; for I am a stranger with You, a sojourner, as all my fathers were."

**Psalm 42:8**

"The Lord will command His lovingkindness in the daytime, and in the night His song shall be with me—a prayer to the God of my life."

**Psalm 119:11**

"Your word I have hidden in my heart, That I might not sin against You."

**Psalm 143:1**

"Hear my prayer, O Lord, give ear to my supplications! In Your faithfulness answer me, And in Your righteousness."

**Jeremiah 29:12**

"Then you will call upon Me and go and pray to Me, and I will listen to you."

**Jeremiah 33:3**

"Call to Me, and I will answer you, and show you great and mighty things, which you do not know."

## Matthew 5:44

"But I say to you, love your enemies, bless those who curse you, do good to those who hate you, and pray for those who spitefully use you and persecute you."

## Matthew 6:6

"But you, when you pray, go into your room, and when you have shut your door, pray to your Father who is in the secret place; and your Father who sees in secret will reward you openly."

## Matthew 17:20-21

"So Jesus said to them, 'Because of your unbelief; for assuredly, I say to you, if you have faith as a mustard seed, you will say to this mountain, "Move from here to there," and it will move; and nothing will be impossible for you. However, this kind does not go out except by prayer and fasting.'"

## Matthew 21:22

"And whatever things you ask in prayer, believing, you will receive."

## Matthew 26:41

"Watch and pray, lest you enter into temptation. The spirit indeed is willing, but the flesh is weak."

## Mark 11:24

"Therefore I say to you, whatever things you ask when you pray, believe that you receive them, and you will have them."

## Mark 11:25

"And whenever you stand praying, if you have anything against anyone, forgive him, that your Father in heaven may also forgive you your trespasses."

### Luke 3:21-22

"When all the people were baptized, it came to pass that Jesus also was baptized; and while He prayed, the heaven was opened. And the Holy Spirit descended in bodily form like a dove upon Him, and a voice came from heaven which said, 'You are My beloved Son; in You I am well pleased.'"

### Luke 6:28

"Bless those who curse you, and pray for those who spitefully use you."

### Luke 18:1

"Then He spoke a parable to them, that men always ought to pray and not lose heart."

### John 20:29

"Jesus said to him, 'Thomas, because you have seen Me, you have believed. Blessed are those who have not seen and yet have believed.'"

### Acts 4:31

"And when they had prayed, the place where they were assembled together was shaken; and they were all filled with the Holy Spirit, and they spoke the word of God with boldness."

### Acts 12:5

"Peter was therefore kept in prison, but constant prayer was offered to God for him by the church."

## Romans 8:26

"Likewise, the Spirit also helps in our weaknesses. For we do not know what we should pray for as we ought, but the Spirit Himself makes intercession for us with groanings which cannot be uttered."

## Romans 12:12

"Rejoicing in hope, patient in tribulation, continuing steadfastly in prayer."

## Ephesians 6:18

"Praying always with all prayer and supplication in the Spirit, being watchful to this end with all perseverance and supplication for all the saints."

## Philippians 1:19

"For I know that this will turn out for my deliverance through your prayer and the supply of the Spirit of Jesus Christ."

## Philippians 4:6

"Be anxious for nothing, but in everything by prayer and supplication, with thanksgiving, let your requests be made known to God."

## Colossians 4:2

"Continue earnestly in prayer, being vigilant in it with thanksgiving."

## 1 Thessalonians 5:17-18

"Pray without ceasing, in everything give thanks; for this is the will of God in Christ Jesus for you."

**James 5:14-15**

"Is anyone among you sick? Let him call for the elders of the church, and let them pray over him, anointing him with oil in the name of the Lord. And the prayer of faith will save the sick, and the Lord will raise him up. And if he has committed sins, he will be forgiven."

**James 5:16**

"Confess your trespasses to one another, and pray for one another, that you may be healed. The effective, fervent prayer of a righteous man avails much."

**1 Peter 3:12**

"For the eyes of the Lord are on the righteous, and His ears are open to their prayers; But the face of the Lord is against those who do evil."

**1 Peter 4:7**

"But the end of all things is at hand; therefore be serious and watchful in your prayers."

**1 John 5:14**

"Now this is the confidence that we have in Him, that if we ask anything according to His will, He hears us."

**3 John 1:2**

"Beloved, I pray that you may prosper in all things and be in health, just as your soul prospers."

# The Model Prayer
# The Lord's Prayer

You should learn, study, and memorize the prayer Jesus taught us to pray. It will set the foundation for your prayer life.

**Matthew 6:5-13**

*"And when you pray, you shall not be like the hypocrites. For they love to pray standing in the synagogues and on the corners of the streets, that they may be seen by men. Assuredly, I say to you, they have their reward. But you, when you pray, go into your room, and when you have shut your door, pray to your Father who is in the secret place; and your Father who sees in secret will reward you openly. And when you pray, do not use vain repetitions as the heathen do. For they think that they will be heard for their many words. "Therefore do not be like them. For your Father knows the things you have need of before you ask Him. In this manner, therefore, pray:*

**Our Father in heaven, Hallowed be Your name. Your kingdom come. Your will be done on earth as it is in heaven. Give us this day our daily bread. And forgive us our debts, as we forgive our debtors. And do not lead us into temptation, but deliver us from the evil one.**

*For Yours is the kingdom and the power and the glory forever. Amen."*

# Day _____

# Thank You for This Day

L ord, I thank You for waking me to see another day. I thank you for breath in my body when some people did not make it to see this day. I realize I may face some things that do not make me feel happy, but I trust in You to give me true joy. Knowing You love me more than I could ever love myself gives me great comfort. It also gives me the strength I need to love others. Help me to be a reflection of Your light to my loved ones and to my fellow man. Each day, allow others to see Christ shining through me and push me to help them smile.

I may get tired but remind me day-by-day that the day is Yours, and it is a blessing for me to experience it. When I focus on this day You have made, I set aside my intentions and ask what You would have me do today. Show me what You require of me today, Lord. Speak to me the desires of Your heart. You made the day, so You have the answers to any questions that may plague my mind. You have the solutions to every issue and concern. Help me, push and drive me to trust in You daily and to simply appreciate the beauty of each day. I realize I will never live this particular day again. For each day holds a blessing set aside, especially for me. So, Father, I thank You for this day and I praise Your name. It is in the name of Jesus Christ I pray, amen.

# Day _____

# Preparation

Lord, I come to you saying, "Thank you for being my Father." I appreciate You for every way You have prepared me up to this point in my life. Teach me to grow in the innermost parts of my being. Aid me in the steps of spiritual growth. Polish my armor of God and cause me to shine as I fight on behalf of my brothers and sisters in Christ. Remind me that my weapons of warfare are not carnal and strongholds can be pulled down and cast away by Your might. Help me tear down bricks that have built up negative thoughts and created barriers in my mind that keep me from speaking Your truth in love and compassion for my fellow man. Help me to always walk in Your ways and to cast mine aside. Give me insight to realize You will always guide me and will never fail me. I desire to trust in You with my whole heart. Teach me each day to do that more and more, dear Lord. Prepare me throughout my body, soul, and spirit for all I will endure and encounter in life. For I know, if I keep my mind stayed on You and Your will, I will never falter without getting back on track. Father, I thank You in advance for preparing me for each day and every experience. It is in the mighty name of Jesus I pray, amen.

## SCRIPTURAL FOCUS

### 2 Corinthians 10:4-6 NKJV

"For the weapons of our warfare are not carnal but mighty in God for pulling down strongholds, casting down arguments and every high thing that exalts itself against the knowledge of God, bringing every thought into captivity to the obedience of Christ, and being ready to punish all disobedience when your obedience is fulfilled."

## SINCERITY NOTES

What are some barriers that have built up negative thoughts in your life?

_____

_____

_____

_____

What are some ways you can fight in the spirit and not in your flesh to overcome those barriers?

_____

_____

_____

_____

Explore some ways the Lord has prepared you for something you experienced recently. How did the Lord prepare you? How did His Word, warning, etc. help you in dealing with the situation?

_____

_____

_____

_____

# Day _____

# Worship

Father, my God, my one and only Lord, I come to You in complete and total surrender. I thank you, Lord, that when I come to You in worship, I am not just expressing a feeling—I am taking time to reverence You in adoration and in honor. Father, I thank You I can come to You just as I am. I appreciate that You know the very hairs on my head, and You know my first day from my last day on this Earth.

God, I praise You for your many works. I praise You for your multiple miracles. God, I praise You for simply being who You are. To use the word "simply" is not good enough, because there is nothing simple about you, Lord. You are the mighty and magnificent Savior. You are the everlasting King. You are the great I AM. You are the God who sent Moses to help free your children. You are the God who numbered Abraham's children as limitless as the stars. You are the one who spoke to the Prophet Elijah and cared for him in his time of despair. You are the God of ages. You are the God who loved us enough to send Your only Son to die for us and rise again to save us from our sins. God, You are mighty and You are wonderful.

The Word asks, "Who is this King of glory?" I respond now as the Word does by saying, "The Lord strong and mighty. The Lord mighty in battle." You are almighty, Father. You are magnificent and excellent. There are not enough adjectives or words to describe You. Father, you are everything. If I could sum it up, I would say, "You are my everything." I call you my everything, because there is nothing I can do apart from You. You are excellent, God. You are the miraculous one, Father. I honor you with respectful devotion today.

I pray as I seek you, God, in obedience; that you know I hold you in the highest regard. You are my Father, and you are my King. You are my Lord, and I worship you. I worship you in the beauty of holiness. For you are right, and You are pure. You are everything that keeps me on the right path and makes my crooked paths straight. You are the One who is holy. You tell us to be holy because You are holy. Lord, I thank you for your holiness.

I thank you that while in worship, I feel your presence. You are near to me. Thank you for the peaceful prayer of worship. Thank you for the quiet stillness of the moment, Father. I thank you for being with me. I honor you, Father. And I take time just to sit and worship You. God, thank you for being with me. Oh, how I love You, Lord. I honor you, my Savior. I adore You and respect you. I appreciate You. I will call out to You and serve you all the days of my life. It is my desire to please you, Lord. It is in Jesus' name I pray, amen.

## SCRIPTURAL FOCUS

### Psalms 96:9

"Oh, worship the Lord in the beauty of holiness! Tremble before Him, all the earth."

### John 4:23-24

"But the hour is coming, and now is, when the true worshipers will worship the Father in spirit and truth; for the Father is seeking such to worship Him. God is Spirit, and those who worship Him must worship in spirit and truth."

## SINCERITY NOTES

The totality of God's power can never be realized, but it can be reverenced. Humbling ourselves in worship is a needed selfless act to honor our Father who loves us. Worshipping God in the beauty of holiness is a way of humbling yourself before Him. Take time to worship Him today.

Some examples of worship: Speaking, praying, praising, shouting, singing, reading God's Word, bowing, lifting hands, standing, dancing, playing instruments, and clapping, etc.

In what ways have you worshipped the Lord in the past?

_____

_____

_____

_____

How did you feel during your time (s) of worship?

_____

_____

_____

_____

How can you worship the Lord today?

_____

_____

_____

_____

# Day _____

# Reading the Bible

I came to understand having scriptures that speak to your situation helps you through hard times. Meditating on His Word opens your ears to the rhythm of the Spirit and tunes your heart to the pulse of heaven. Pairing the reading of His Word with the power of prayer will turn some things around in your life.

As I read the Bible and prayed more, the Lord revealed hidden treasures in the Spirit. The Lord spoke one day.

*"My Word is a light. It illuminates scars and heals souls. It corrects behaviors and convicts broken places in the mind. My Word can reach anyone if only they eat it and feast on its richness. It illuminates in darkness and shines brightest in chaos for those who desire freedom. Find me, and I will pull you out of pitiful places, dungeon-directed captivity and soul-freezing mentalities."*

That spoke to me deeply and resonated in my soul and spirit. I pray it helps you as well.

Father God, Lord Jesus, I thank you for waking me to see this day. Thank you for helping me to get up and get moving. I thank you for completeness in my mind. God, I thank you for the fullness in my body. Lord, as I move forward, I ask that you give me clear insight. Holy Spirit, I honor you. Holy Spirit, I ask as I read the Word of God that you give me insight, understanding, and clarity. Please be with me. Remove all the distractions in my path. Block out anything that would keep me or hinder me from hearing God's Word.

Help the Word of God resonate with me first, and then help me relate to it. Give me clear revelation and help the words come alive on the pages. I ask that You spiritually illuminate things, so I can see clearly and can understand what the authors meant under Your divine inspiration, God. I know the Word is God-breathed, and I am asking You to flow upon me. Give me fresh understanding as clear wind. Give me new insights as you see fit. Every time I open the Word of God, help me learn something new and not take it for granted. Help me not to focus solely on what I have learned before, but to put it together with what You are giving me now.

Help me understand this is something I need to do. Help me not to read the Word out of obligation but help me to read the Word out of commitment to You. Help me to read the Word out of a yearning and a desire to grow closer to You and to hear Your words more clearly. Help me sit in front of the Word and feast on Your Word as fresh manna. Feed me each morsel of scripture. God, activate a fire within me, so I long for the Word, and am happy about reading the Word You provided for my spiritual maturity. God, I thank you that I have this guide book as I live out each day of my life. I thank You for taking time to care for me and provide for me with intricate detail.

Lord, You spoke words to the authors of old so I could have words to guide me in daily living. God, I know some may say everything is not explicitly laid out in the Bible. Lord, help me understand that even if it is not spelled out uniquely in individual words, something in Your Word applies to every situation. There is something in Your Word that guides us in many different areas. For that, I thank You. I thank You for the things that are literal. I thank You for the things that are figurative. I thank You for the things based on customs and principles and for the things yet to come. Help me study so I understand the times and places in the context of which the Word was written. Father, help me not to read just one scripture. Help me put it together with other scriptures, so I can get a full and well-rounded contextual understanding of the Word. Help me go back and relate to other scriptures that speak about the portion of text I am studying.

God, I know You came not to abolish the law, but to fulfill it. Father, I know there is a New Testament I can reflect upon, and I can grow from. God, I know there is an Old Testament that shows us the great I AM, and that prophesies of the coming of Your only begotten son, my Savior, Jesus Christ. I thank You because Your Word speaks of You and gives me insight into the fact that Jesus came to save me.

I thank You, Jesus, for saving me. I thank You for the New Testament where you are revealed to me. I thank you for Your life as an example. Father, help me be diligent and consistent in reading Your Word and give me what I need to understand Your Word.

Jesus, thank You for leaving me a Comforter. Holy Spirit, I invite You into this atmosphere. Please speak to me. Please show me what I should glean from the Word. Please be with me throughout my reading today. I ask You to open my heart and mind in areas where they are closed. Help me not to be stubborn about what I think I know, but to be open about what You know. Please be with me, God, throughout this process.

God, I thank You in advance for right understanding. I ask that You help me not to keep this Word to myself but to share it with others. Help me speak a word to someone else that may give them comfort. Help me study, so the Word may be hidden in my heart. God, I thank You for this process, and I thank You for the opportunity to read Your Word. Thank You for this private time with You. I do not take it for granted. It is in Jesus' name I pray, amen.

## SCRIPTURAL FOCUS

### Psalms 119:11

"Your word I have hidden in my heart, That I might not sin against You."

**Isaiah 40:8**

"The grass withers, the flower fades, but the word of our God stands forever."

**2 Timothy 2:15**

"Be diligent to present yourself approved to God, a worker who does not need to be ashamed, rightly dividing the word of truth."

**Hebrews 4:12**

"For the word of God is living and powerful, and sharper than any two-edged sword, piercing even to the division of soul and spirit, and of joints and marrow, and is a discerner of the thoughts and intents of the heart."

## SINCERITY NOTES

We have access to the Word of God on every hand. With so many outlets to access the Word, we have no excuse to go without dedicating time to the Lord. We make time for what we value as important. Open your Bible, listen to or view a podcast, read/listen to a devotional, tune in on social media, listen to a CD, watch a DVD, download a mp3, tablet or phone, etc.

Maybe it is in your heart to make time to read the Bible, but you have not dedicated yourself to it yet. Today is a great day to start. Lack of knowledge is a silent killer of spiritual growth. Are you giving life to your spirit?

———

I can read my Bible more if I

_____

_____

_____

_____

Today, I commit to reading at least _____ scripture(s) a day. I will work up to _____ scriptures a day. I realize if I miss a day, I can start again the next day without guilt or a fear of reprisal from the Lord. The Lord I serve does not operate in that manner. He will give me comfort as I press forward on this journey of learning His Word.

# Day _____

# Giving

Lord, I come to You saying thank You. Thank You for everything You have provided for me. I thank You for every day that You have been my supplier and the great provider of all that has kept me going. Father, I thank You that I am not in a place I cannot come back from. I thank You I have everything I need. Father, even in the times when I feel as if I do not have everything I desire, I realize I do not live in lack.

Your Word tells me You will supply all of my needs according to Your riches and glory. Father, I thank You for being that provider. I ask You to help me in the area of giving and tithing, Father. I want to be a good steward. Mature me into a good steward over everything You have given to me. Help me, Lord, to give You my firstfruits. Help me follow the example of Abel in the Bible and give You what is Yours first.

God, I thank You that even though sometimes I may fall short, You are there to teach me how to do and be better. You are there to guide me. You are there to pick me up. I thank You for never condemning me but gently urging my spirit to get back on track.

Help me, Father, as I move forward in the area tithing. I may not always be strong, but I always have a desire and motivation to serve You. God increase that desire and strengthen the motivation. Also, Lord, help me be a giver. Help me sow into good ground. Help me experience "you reap what you sow," and if I give plentifully, I will reap plentifully.

I don't want to give out of necessity or begrudgingly. I want to give because it is honorable and because it is right. Your Word tells me You love a cheerful giver. So, Father, create in me a right heart to cheerfully give to You first. I even ask, Lord, that You help me with finances and with my increase, so I will be able to give without any hesitation. Help me live within my means and not to stretch further than what I need at any time or during any season of life.

I thank you, God, and I believe I am a lender and not a borrower. I believe I am the head and not the tail. I believe out of my hands shall flow supply and demand, and increase will be established over my life. I trust You to allow me to live prosperous in every area of my life. God, I trust You with my all. Please do all I have asked and more according to Your will. It is in the name of Jesus I pray, amen.

## SCRIPTURAL FOCUS

### Malachi 3:10-11

"'Bring all the tithes into the storehouse, that there may be food in My house, and try Me now in this'" says the Lord of hosts, 'If I will not open for you the windows of heaven and pour out for you such blessing that there will not be room enough to receive it. And I will rebuke the devourer for your sakes, so that he will not destroy the fruit of your ground, nor shall the vine fail to bear fruit for you in the field,' says the Lord of hosts."

### Luke 6:38

"Give, and it will be given to you: good measure, pressed down, shaken together, and running over will be put into your bosom. For with the same measure that you use, it will be measured back to you."

**2 Corinthians 9:6-7**

"But this I say: 'He who sows sparingly will also reap sparingly, and he who sows bountifully will also reap bountifully. So let each one give as he purposes in his heart, not grudgingly or of necessity; for God loves a cheerful giver.'"

## SINCERITY NOTES

Give with the right intention in your heart. When you give, do it without the expectation of receiving anything in return. We do not give to receive from man. God supplies you with blessings according to His will. Give as unto God. You should be giving to honor Him, anyway. Giving to a person is not a means of showing how much you can bless them. It should be about showing them God answers prayer. People do not pray to you—they pray to God. He uses you as a vessel to do His will. It is important to keep our giving in perspective.

When I give, my heart is

_____

_____

_____

_____

Give an assignment to your tithe/seed/gift. I command my seed to

_____

_____

_____

# Day _____

# Service

Lord, I thank You for this day. Thank You for the peace in my heart and in my mind. I also thank You for the calm in my spirit, Father. There are so many things going through my mind, but I call all of them to quiet down so I may hear you clearly. Please blot out any distractions, remove any hindrances, and allow me to hear You with razor sharp clarity.

Today, Holy Spirit, I invite You in. I invite You into this atmosphere to commune with me and offer guidance. Jesus, I thank You for Your sacrifice. I thank You for Your peace that surrounds me. Thank You for the protection that comforts me.

Lord, today, I am Your humble servant. How can I serve You, God? What can I do for You today? I do not ask because You need me. You have everything at the palm of Your hand. You can do whatever You will, but I thank You for using me. Lord, show me who I can pray for today. Show me who I can call. Show me who I can message. Place those on my heart who need a special touch today. God, place those on my heart who are in need of prayer today. Remind me, Lord, of those who I have told I would pray for them, but it slipped my mind. Forgive me, God, for not stopping to pray when I said I would. Lord, please stop me and help me remember the world. There are so many people hurting throughout the world. God, I'm asking you to cover them and be where I cannot be. Help where I am unable to help. Meet their needs like only You can, Lord.

Please speak to me now, God—and as you speak, I will be silent. I will listen for what You have for me to do today. Help me focus on hearing You. In the name of Jesus I pray, amen.

## SCRIPTURAL FOCUS

### Psalms 100:2

"Serve the Lord with gladness; come before His presence with singing."

### John 12:26

"If anyone serves Me, let him follow Me; and where I am, there My servant will be also. If anyone serves Me, him My Father will honor."

### Ephesians 6:7-8

"With goodwill doing service, as to the Lord, and not to men, knowing that whatever good anyone does, he will receive the same from the Lord, whether he is a slave or free."

## SINCERITY NOTES

I just believe God is real, alive, and loves us all. That's real love. God is so amazing. He will open doors you never noticed were there. Be open to being a willing vessel and watch Him use you. In case you're doubting yourself, let me be the first to say, "Yes you can!"

# Day _____

## Focus

Father, I come to you right now thanking You for this day. Father, I need You today. I have a lot on my plate and a great deal I will encounter. I do not know how to prepare for any of it; and quite frankly, I do not know how to face it. I know Your Word assures me You will not leave me nor forsake me. I am trusting You to be with me, because I cannot make it without You. Every day has a new struggle and a new obstacle to overcome, but I know I can make it with You pulling me through it all. Thank You for being my lifeguard and thank You for the ability to be in my right mind. Father, I thank You for being with me, even when I feel like I am just moving in different directions. I thank You, God, for who You are my life.

Lord, I am coming to You today because of an area I have been struggling with. I know we are supposed to speak those things that are not as though they were, and we are supposed to look at the good things. God, although I see the good, I have been overwhelmed with maintaining my focus. Some days, I cannot seem to get one thing done without my mind going in different directions. Other days, I am not thinking about anything at all, but I cannot will myself to get anything done. I may spend hours sitting, thinking about nothing, doing nothing, and trying to will myself to get things done. But I just cannot get anything done. Father, this bothers me deeply, because I want to be a good steward of my time. I want to be productive in a day. I want to get things done. I want to please You, and I want to be there for my family and for kingdom work.

Lord, I ask You to help me in this area. I know there is an end to it, because You are a God who hears me when I call. God, I know there is a purpose to this battle, but I really do not know that purpose. When I think about the purpose, or when I try to figure out the intent, I do not have the answers, and I wonder if this is just a season for me. Is it something I am going through? Are You teaching me how to wait on You more? I do not know, Father, so I am asking You—speak to me. Show me and tell me if there is anything in my heart that needs to be removed. Father, please reveal it to me. Anything I have done to open the door to this hindrance, please remove it. Father, forgive me and seal it shut with the blood of the Lamb. I am asking You to help me in this area, because I know when this area gets cleared up, it will aid in other areas of my life—like time, stability, and stewardship. God, I want to be right in each area, so I'm asking You to help me. God, show me day-by-day and give me the strength to keep fighting so I will have laser sharp focus and, I will be able to get things done. "Thank you God," because I will overcome this battle. I thank you, God, and I praise You in advance for deliverance. It is in Jesus' mighty name I pray, amen.

## SCRIPTURAL FOCUS

### Proverbs 4:25

"Let your eyes look straight ahead, and your eyelids look right before you."

### Isaiah 26:3

"You will keep him in perfect peace, whose mind is stayed on You, because he trusts in You."

**Philippians 4:8**

"Finally, brethren, whatever things are true, whatever things are noble, whatever things are just, whatever things are pure, whatever things are lovely, whatever things are of good report, if there is any virtue and if there is anything praiseworthy—meditate on these things."

## SINCERITY NOTES

No matter what you face today, remember you are not fighting on your own. In fact, you're not even fighting. The battle is not yours; it is the Lords! GOD is everywhere, especially inside of you. There are NO limits to what you can do.

Try setting a timer and focusing for 15 minutes, 30 minutes, 45 minutes, or an hour at a time. Start where you need to and note your progress.

_____

_____

_____

_____

Are there distractions around you? What can you do to eliminate them?

_____

_____

_____

_____

Celebrate the small victory each time you have a good day of focus. Today,
I celebrate myself because

_____

_____

_____

_____

# Day _____

# Faith

Lord, please strengthen my faith. I know many people believe in You but do not have a relationship with You. I know plenty of family and friends who believe in You without cultivating a relationship with You. I have been in that place before, but I thank You for showing me the right way. A relationship with You creates a bond with growing and developing feelings and desires. As I grow and spend more time with You, I do not only have feelings for You, but I want to talk to You and spend more time with You. Lord, I desire a deeper spiritual intimacy with You. Even when You are close, I want to feel You closer. I want to be held by You so I am truly comforted. I need to know even more that You care for me. I also want You to know I care for You. Lord, increase my faith in You when I am in doubt and I lack trust You will come through for me. I know I will not always know the outcome of things, but teach me to trust You, the author and finisher of my faith, know all. Trusting You and having faith in Your power is how I heal from my broken places on the inside.

Lord, help me stay in a place of seeking Your face. I want never to get enough of You. I want to love Your Word so much that it never grows old. As a matter of fact, Lord, please allow it to become more enlightening every time I read it. Every time I hear Your voice, allow me to soak in every word. I want to listen intently to Your will for my life.

When I am lacking faith, I feel like You are not there, and I am lost and incomplete. I know that is a lack of faith and unrighteous thinking, because, I can never be disconnected from Your love. I may not always hear

You or feel You near, but You are ALWAYS with me. Hebrews 13:5 tells me You said, "I will never leave you nor forsake you."

When I cling fast to this promise from You, my weariness dries up, and my faith in You is ignited. God help me remember Your words when my faith is lacking. The enemy would love to see me empty, but God, You have filled me up and healed my sin-sick and suffering soul. Thank You in advance for the faith to keep pressing forward and thank You for renewing my trust in You. You are my faithful Savior, and I love You. It is in the faithful name of Jesus I pray, amen.

## SCRIPTURAL FOCUS

### John 20:29

"Jesus said to him, 'Thomas, because you have seen Me, you have believed. Blessed are those who have not seen and yet have believed.'"

### 2 Corinthians 5:7

"For we walk by faith, not by sight.

### Hebrews 11:1

"Now faith is the substance of things hoped for, the evidence of things not seen."

## SINCERITY NOTES

Faith is about what you cannot see. Your physical eyes will lie to you, but your spiritual eyes are marksman sharp every time you listen to the Holy Spirit. What you cannot see physically guards your life and keeps you breathing. Jesus is always there.

In what area do you lack faith? Why do you doubt?

_____

_____

_____

_____

Are you trusting, believing, and exercising your faith daily? How?

_____

_____

_____

_____

In what way(s) are you working to increase your faith?

_____

_____

_____

# Day _____

# Selfishness

Lord, only You know what is truly in my heart. Impart to me what is right and root out what is wrong. Cause me to hear You and live for You in a more earnest and true way.

Cleanse me of selfish thoughts and intentions and mold me into a vessel of Your will. Help me suit up daily for battle and cause my soul to war against my flesh. Help me be open and willing to help those who are in need and not to turn a blind eye to pain and suffering. Help me to be renewed daily in You.

Lord, today I ask You to deplete me totally of a self-serving nature. Empty me of the parts of myself that cause me to rely on myself and avoid looking to You for true help. Cleanse me of the parts that do not look anything like You. Strengthen those places that barely resemble You. Increase the areas within me that honor and revere You. Make me and mold me in the manner to which You see fit. I pray I will not rebel against Your will.

Lord, show me how not to only think about being more, but to have the drive to become more without coveting what someone else obtained. Help me get past the status quo of religion and cause me to gravitate toward the realness of right relationship with Christ. Lord, save me from me and bond me with You.

Lord, teach me to walk in life daily for Your glory. Take away selfish intentions and the desire to be seen or noticed. Make it clear what You need from me and cause me to be a willing vessel. Help me rest in the purpose of what it means to "do it for your glory." Help me walk in love and reserve judgement for the Lord. I realize things are not always as they seem, and I need to see others through Your lens. Help me not to look only with the physical eye but to see things with a spiritual heart.

This is a time to open my spiritual eyes and unclog my natural ear gates. Warfare is real, and I am in the thick of it. Help me put on my armor, get in Your Word, pray, and be prepared at all times. I can stand against a real enemy who wants to see me fall if I continue to stand with You. There is NO OTHER WAY. This is my prayer today. In the way-making name of Jesus I pray, amen.

## SCRIPTURAL FOCUS

### Romans 12:3

"For I say, through the grace given to me, to everyone who is among you, not to think of himself more highly than he ought to think, but to think soberly, as God has dealt to each one a measure of faith."

### Philippians 2:3-5

"Let nothing be done through selfish ambition or conceit, but in lowliness of mind let each esteem others better than himself. Let each of you look out not only for his own interests but also for the interests of others."

## SINCERITY NOTES

God gives to you and not the other way around. He gives to everyone according to His will. Do not look at someone who you perceive as having less and think you are better than them. Your idea of less may be God's best in their lives. Remain humble and display humility.

Be honest and name a time when you have been selfish.

_____

_____

_____

_____

Do you still struggle in this area? Why/ Why not?

_____

_____

_____

_____

Has anyone been selfish toward you? How did it make you feel? Did you pray about it? Did you pray until you overcame the hurt?

_____

_____

_____

_____

# Day _____

# Self-Worth

Lord, I thank You, Father, for taking the time to make me in Your image. Thank You for carving out time to choose what I would look like, what my soul would be, and how my spirit would be. Father, you even chose how my body would come into this world. I thank You for choosing my parents and family. I express thanks for You knowing my beginning from my end. Father, You are the author and the finisher of my faith. So, I thank you, Lord, for creating me. I thank You for considering me to even have life. God, thank You for knowing the very hairs on my head. I thank You for knowing the number of days I will be here in this life until You call me back to be with You in eternity.

I'm here on this Earth, Lord, and sometimes I deal with my flesh. Lord, in dealing with my flesh, sometimes I do not like what I see. I know that is not good, because if I am created in Your image, I should look at myself and beyond myself and see You. Lord, I also know I should be grateful for everything about myself because You took time to fashion me. Lord, help me see the beauty in myself. Help me see what You see when You look at me and allow me a glimpse of myself through Your eyes. Help me believe what Your Word says—*I am fearfully and wonderfully made.* Help me believe You created me to be your crowning creation.

I know You created me as an example of Your love—so when I look at myself, I should be viewing a reflection of Your love, which is right, true, and pure love. Lord, I am thankful for so many things about myself. I am glad I am in my right mind, and I am glad I have some sense of health in my body. Father, appreciative I have the faculty of my limbs when many do not. So, I thank You for everything You have already done for me.

Lord, I have confidence there will be a turnaround. Equalize my mind so I can get to the place where I love what I see. I love who You created, but I do not always love the me I see. So help me, Lord, to overcome. Help me get through these struggles and battles. Help me know I am indeed fearfully and wonderfully made, because I was formed by You. God, I have faith in You for healing in this area. I will diligently do my part to triumph over my mind and negative thoughts. I honor You as a God who exchanges sadness for joy. My joy is on the way! It is in the glorious name of Jesus I pray, amen.

## SCRIPTURAL FOCUS

### Psalms 139:14

"I will praise You, for I am fearfully and wonderfully made; marvelous are Your works, and that my soul knows very well."

### Philippians 4:13

"I can do all things through Christ who strengthens me."

### Nehemiah 8:10

"Do not sorrow, for the joy of the LORD is your strength."

## SINCERITY NOTES

It is important to know your worth. Encourage yourself to be the best you can be. You are more than enough for anybody or anyone that comes into your life. Continue to grow and be molded for the good of God. You are priceless. Stop tormenting yourself and walk in victory.

What is something I do not like about myself?

_____

_____

_____

_____

How can I work on it?

_____

_____

_____

_____

What is one thing I love about myself?

_____

_____

_____

_____

Take the thing you love and build on it. Tell yourself something positive every day and grow from there. You will begin to love yourself through the heart of God.

# Day _____

# Connections with Others

Dear Lord, please cover me and everyone connected to me. I ask You to let them know You hold them in the comfort of Your care. Please help them overcome every attack, obstacle, and test that comes their way. Please help them take the high road that leads to You and not get stuck in the pit of the valley. Help them transcend mountains and soar with the eagles. Put a fire of right-thinking and perseverance in their spirit that allows them to break through spiritual barriers. Help them press through with power and praise. Allow them to experience victory and joy in You.

Lord, also cover the connections I need to be separated from and forgive me for not distancing myself when you urged me to. Help me more quickly realize all connections are not from You, and some people and things I am holding on to are blocking my ability to receive the right connections You have stored up for me. Help me with releasing when I clench tightly onto those things. Help me to walk away when my flesh tells me it would be more pleasing to stay.

Lord, speak to me clearly and show me the difference between blessed bonds and chaotic connections. I trust You to speak and help me hear with a discerning ear. Thank You for clarity, Lord. It is in the mighty name of Jesus I pray, amen.

## SCRIPTURAL FOCUS

### Job 42:10

"And the Lord restored Job's losses when he prayed for his friends. Indeed, the Lord gave Job twice as much as he had before."

### Proverbs 27:17

"As iron sharpens iron, so a man sharpens the countenance of his friend."

### Romans 12:16-18

"Be of the same mind toward one another. Do not set your mind on high things but associate with the humble. Do not be wise in your own opinion. Repay no one evil for evil. Have regard for good things in the sight of all men. If it is possible, as much as depends on you, live peaceably with all men."

## SINCERITY NOTES

We are relational beings, and our relationships should be based on our relationship with God. The connection to our Father sets the stage for what we allow and do not allow. Take a moment to look at how and why you spend time in His presence.

_____

_____

_____

Lord, do I have any connections that need to be severed? What is the Holy Spirit revealing to you?

_____

_____

_____

_____

Lord, what connections am I overlooking that need strengthening? What is the Holy Spirit revealing to you?

_____

_____

_____

_____

# Day _____

# When People Hurt You

Lord, Heavenly Father, Great Redeemer, Almighty Savior, Blessed Peacemaker, All Powerful God, Holy One, I Am, Great Physician—I look to You now to heal me from the inside out. I am seeking You to nourish those places in my heart that are in a deadened stance. Restore to me a mindset that reflects Your character. Heal my ailments—mentally, emotionally and physically. Help me see if I hold the death of hurt and pain in my heart and mind, it will have an effect on my body—inside and outside. I do not want to hurt anymore, Father.

Call me back toward your ways. Remind me You are coming back, and I need to be ready. I cannot be ready to fight in your army or to stand in any battle like this, Lord. A part of me feels broken. Pain has held me back for too long. Forgive me, Lord, where I have fallen short. Help me no longer meet people and put up walls out of previous hurt, but instead to uplift my fellow man. Free me from an unhealthy self-mentality and cause me to look at the kingdom as one body of Christ with many moving parts. Help me work freely as a part of that body without reservations and to trust completely in You. Implore me to embrace Your children and not lash out because of my painful experiences. Help me not to live in a state of offense and be on the defense only to the attacks of the enemy.

I desire to be whole and functional in all aspects of my life. I trust You, my Savior, to help me and give me the strength to stand in Your strength. Please do it, Lord, and show me clearly when I am heading in the wrong direction. Only You can heal me and make me whole. In the marvelous and healing name of Jesus I pray, amen.

## SCRIPTURAL FOCUS

### Matthew 5:44

"But I say to you, love your enemies, bless those who curse you, do good to those who hate you, and pray for those who spitefully use you and persecute you,"

### Luke 6:28

"Bless those who curse you, and pray for those who spitefully use you."

### Romans 12:17-19

"Repay no one evil for evil. Have regard for good things in the sight of all men. If it is possible, as much as depends on you, live peaceably with all men. Beloved, do not avenge yourselves, but rather give place to wrath; for it is written, 'Vengeance is Mine, I will repay,' says the Lord."

## SINCERITY NOTES

People who are hurting will oftentimes look and act like someone or something other than who you know them to be. Instead of lashing out at them, pray for their healing. Remember not to engage in an un-Christlike manner and resist a tit-for-tat response, because you cannot fight a spirit with the flesh. As a warrior for the kingdom of God, you have to understand this principle. You also have to know when to back away and turn them over to the Lord. Set your healthy boundaries and remember to protect your peace.

Even when you do not want to pray for people, whom prayer seems too good for, you have to obey the Word of God. The Lord knew we would struggle in this area, and He equipped us for the battle. How people treat you is their business. How you respond or react is your business. Dealing with both is God's business. He always has you covered.

Who hurt you?

_____

_____

_____

_____

Have you prayed about the situation and asked God to help?

_____

_____

_____

_____

If no, why not?

_____

_____

_____

_____

Have you forgiven them?

_____

_____

_____

_____

If no, why not?

_____

_____

_____

_____

Do you have peace about the situation?

_____

_____

_____

If not, pray for peace. Father, today I seek You for my peace. I am asking

_____

_____

_____

_____

What boundaries will you set? What will you do to stick to them once they are set?

_____

_____

_____

_____

**Note:** *If your issue is deep-rooted in trauma and you are already praying, do not hesitate to seek professional help as well. Professional care and prayer are powerful tools for your total healing.*

# Day _____

# Forgiveness

*It has to hurt before it can heal. If not, it will hinder you*
*and hold you hostage. Walk through it and be totally free.*

SJJ

Father, I thank you. I appreciate You for loving and forgiving me of all of my sins. Lord, I humbly bow before You, because I know there is unforgiveness in my heart. What I have endured in life, and what some people have done to me, has made my heart harden in certain areas. I can go out and smile. I can love on people. I can even make it through without people noticing the truth. However, I am holding something hard around my heart, Lord. There is a cage that exists there, keeping parts of me bound. I desperately want to be totally free.

Lord, I ask that You help me take this thing I have been holding on to that is hurting me. Please take it, remove it, and give me healing in that area. Give me peace, Lord. Help it to no longer overpower me. Help it not to be like a thorn in my flesh. God, I know your grace is sufficient, but this is extremely hard. I am struggling with this, and I know You would have me forgive, Father. I am supposed to forgive because You forgive us. Help me Lord just to let this go! I have been holding on so long the weight of it feels unbearable. It is starting to weigh me down both mentally and physically. I can see the effects of unforgiveness coming out in situations where my body is resisting, and it is not healing. Father, I am asking You to take this load. Please take it and lighten it for me.

Show me how to forgive. Show me how to move on. Lord, help me understand forgiveness does not mean I have to give access to people or situations that seek to hurt or harm me. It does not mean I have to allow people who intentionally hurt me back into my life. Lord, teach me safe and healthy boundaries so I can have the protection I need.

Father, please teach me, because I want to do better. I want to be better. I have a strong yearning within me to be better. I want to forgive easily. Lord, please help me in this area. I know as long as I am diligent and as long as I am willing and have faith, You will see me through. I thank You, Lord, for a release in my heart, mind, soul, and spirit. God, I praise You in advance for my total and complete healing. It is in Jesus' name I pray, amen.

## SCRIPTURAL FOCUS

### Matthew 6:12

"And forgive us our debts, As we forgive our debtors."

### Mark 11:25

"And whenever you stand praying, if you have anything against anyone, forgive him, that your Father in heaven may also forgive you your trespasses."

### Ephesians 4:31-32

"Let all bitterness, wrath, anger, clamor, and evil speaking be put away from you, with all malice. And be kind to one another, tenderhearted, forgiving one another, even as God in Christ forgave you."

# SINCERITY NOTES

Christ forgave you. We must forgive others because Christ forgave us first. Even when people treat you badly, remember it happened to Him first. The Lord showed you how to walk upright and love your brothers and sisters (all races, religions and backgrounds). Forgiveness is key because you deserve to have peace.

When you walk through one or several fragmented relationships, it can lead you down a stormy and tumultuous road that can cause you to miss hearing the direction of the Lord if you harbor resentment and/or unforgiveness. In addition, you can lose a huge part of yourself if you are not careful. Take time to pray and heal. Allow time to commune with the Lord and ask Him to remove any unhealed places. Repent for any unforgiveness you are harboring in your heart. God is faithful, patient, and kind, and He will be there when you are ready.

I have not forgiven _____

because _____.

I will take these steps to forgive

_____

_____

_____

_____

Father, please help me take the steps I have laid out and give me the strength to follow through with them daily until I am able to totally forgive. I realize this is necessary for me to be and feel whole.

# Day _____

# Right Words

F ather, Your Word tells us creatures can be tamed, but no man can tame the tongue. Lord, please help me to train my tongue by speaking Your Word. Allow no negative words to exit my lips and permit no sinful thoughts to enter my mind. Cause me to think upon others through the love You have shown me. Your love is my example, and I strive to be like You in all my ways. Cause me to think before I speak and to listen and discern much more than I talk or react. Teach me the difference between responding in a Christlike manner and reacting out of my flesh. Slow my feelings toward offense and cause me not to live in a posture of defensiveness.

Strengthen my heart to identify with the good in Your people and not to reflect too eagerly on the past hurts that have scarred me over time. Make my speech resemble Your words whispered to me in prayer. Remind me of the grace and mercy You showed to me, even when I was wrong. Help me show that same type of compassion to everyone I come in contact with daily. Keep me from relying on anger and instead, impart to me ways to slay the unruly nature that sometimes tries to rise up. Please settle those emotions and remind me I am Your child and must act accordingly. Help me pray for my fellow brothers and sisters instead of lashing them with my tongue. As You strengthen me, I understand my part is to actively work on my responses and to meditate on Your Word so it will be hidden in my heart and flow from my lips. In the capable name of Jesus I pray, amen.

# SCRIPTURAL FOCUS

## Matthew 12:36

"But I say to you that for every idle word men may speak, they will give account of it in the day of judgment."

## James 3:7-10 NKJV

"For every kind of beast and bird, of reptile and creature of the sea, is tamed and has been tamed by mankind. But no man can tame the tongue. It is an unruly evil, full of deadly poison. With it we bless our God and Father, and with it we curse men, who have been made in the similitude of God. Out of the same mouth proceed blessing and cursing. My brethren, these things ought not to be so."

# SINCERITY NOTES

*You will never escape your mental prison if chains keep falling out of your mouth. What you speak can keep you in bondage or set you free.*

SJJ

I am a good/great/okay/not so good (circle one) listener. I would be a better listener if I

_____

_____

_____

I can work on speaking life to others by

I can work on speaking life to myself by

# Day _____

# Brokenness

God, I need you right now. I come to you broken and not knowing where all the pieces of me have been left. I have been going so long with a smile on my face, and no one saw the pain hidden beneath it all. It has been a tough road, and I do not know which way to turn. Today, I proclaim anything broken will be mended. I pray anything hanging on by a fiber will be strengthened. I pray all my unbelief will be replaced with hope. I pray I find the substance of that hope by clinging fast to Your faith, Lord.

Lord, I am asking You to cover everyone who has a full or heavy heart, and I also ask for filling in my broken state. Bless me to cast all my cares upon You, because I know You care for me. Even being armed with that knowledge, I still cannot shake this feeling of being lost within myself. Help me know even more that You are a God of many names—way-maker, King of glory, Jehovah-Jireh, Miracle-worker, Healer, Yahweh, Elohim, Adonai, Mighty Counselor, King of kings and so much more. I can call on You in my time of distress, and You will surely answer. You can do all things and handle anything that comes to keep me bound.

I pray for a change of heart today, because my heart is hurting from a deep place. I pray a refreshing in the spirit. I pray for a breakthrough and a release in my soul that seems scarred and wounded. Your powerful Word tells me You are near to those who have a broken heart. Be near to me, Father, because my heart is broken. No matter how I feel, I know You are able to heal and mend all the broken pieces and make me whole. Please do it for me, Lord, and I will testify of Your glory. It is in the mighty name of Jesus I pray, amen.

## SCRIPTURAL FOCUS

### Psalms 34:18

"The Lord is near to those who have a broken heart and saves such as have a contrite spirit."

### Psalms 147:3

"He heals the brokenhearted and binds up their wounds."

### 2 Cor. 12:9

"And He said to me, 'My grace is sufficient for you, for My strength is made perfect in weakness.' Therefore, most gladly I will rather boast in my infirmities, that the power of Christ may rest upon me."

## SINCERITY NOTES

*There is a young girl inside of every woman and a young boy inside of every man who has endured various trials in life. The confusion comes in when we allow that inner child to speak up when a grown-up response is needed. Don't let those broken places from childhood cause you to live your adult life in pieces. True peace is attainable through Christ.*

SJJ

It is tough when a breakthrough is attached to a breaking point. Just know God is breaking up the chaotic places so the blessings can break forth. The good news is you will not break down.

Have you ever felt broken? When?

_____

_____

_____

_____

What steps can you take to overcome how you feel?

_____

_____

_____

_____

God does not want anything from you more than He wants you to love Him with your whole heart, soul, and mind. He desires to clean up what is in your heart and make it new. He is a Master mender. Take all the shattered fragments of your life and give them to Him. Give it to Him today, because He knows exactly what you need. Trust Him.

# Day _____

# Worry and Anxiety

Lord, today I need you. I can feel anxiety lurking, like it wants to tap on my shoulder. I do not know why, and I do not understand why I am feeling so anxious. I am not a person who worries. I am not a person who fears. I do not fear because Your Word tells me You have not given me the spirit of fear, but one of power, love, and a sound mind. Your Word also tells me to be anxious for nothing, but in everything by prayer and supplication, with thanksgiving, to let my requests be made known to God. Yahweh, right now, make my request known to You through this prayer. Please God, help me not to be attacked by the feeling of anxiety. Help me not to give in to the pressures all around me.

God, help me to keep pushing forward—not because what I feel is invalid, but because the extent of what I am feeling is more than I have the ability to take on. I know Your Word also tells me I can cast my cares upon You because You care for me. So, God, help me rest in that care. Help me find comfort in that care. Help me feel surrounded by Your care. God infuse me in the very luxury of Your care. Father, I trust You, I honor You, and I thank you for being there for me. I know anxiety is not my portion. I know worry is not my portion. Lord, help me take one day at a time, because right now, that is all I can handle. I do not have to worry about tomorrow, because tomorrow has enough worries of its own.

Help me stand in today and take one hour at a time, or even one minute at a time if I have to. God, please reassure me within my spirit that at each step and in each moment, You will be there with me at every turn. I love and appreciate You. I thank You that even as I am praying this prayer, the feeling of anxiety and worry are lifting right now. I believe it in the name of Jesus! It shall not be otherwise, because when I ask something of You, I have to stand strong, expecting you are going to turn things around. I know that You, Father God, will do it. Thank You. I honor You, I believe I am better, and I trust I will continue to improve day-by-day. I will not give up because my hope is in You. Thank you, God, for the relief. In the name of Jesus I pray, amen.

## SCRIPTURAL FOCUS

### Matthew 6:26-27

"Look at the birds of the air, for they neither sow nor reap nor gather into barns; yet your heavenly Father feeds them. Are you not of more value than they? Which of you by worrying can add one cubit to his stature?"

### Matthew 6:34

"Therefore do not worry about tomorrow, for tomorrow will worry about its own things. Sufficient for the day is its own trouble."

### Philippians 4:6

"Be anxious for nothing, but in everything by prayer and supplication, with thanksgiving, let your requests be made known to God."

### 2 Timothy 1:7

"For God has not given us a spirit of fear, but of power and of love and of a sound mind."

## SINCERITY NOTES

I get anxious and worried when

_____

_____

_____

_____

I realize anxiety is not healthy for me—mentally, physically, or spiritually. In my prayer time, I hear the Lord saying

_____

_____

_____

_____

God knows exactly what I need when I need it. Lord, please remind me daily that You are bigger than anything I may face. I do not have to worry or be anxious about what tomorrow holds, because God knows the beginning from the end. He knows what I will face, and He is already waiting to hear me when I call on Him. I will not allow my troubles to consume me or be afraid of what they may bring with them. Anxiety does not provide me with a resting place. My peace is found in Him.

# Day _____

# Rest

Dear Lord, thank you for another opportunity to come to you. Father, You know where I have been daily. You know how I have been up at night. And You know how I have been lacking sleep with thoughts in my mind that seem never to turn off. Rest escapes me lately as I cannot seem to close my eyes long enough to feel at ease. I thank you, Lord, for peace in my spirit, but I realize there is something unaddressed. Father, please give me some insight. Open my heart and my spiritual eyes to see what is hindering my rest.

Father, I desire rest—for Jesus showed us in Your Word there are times He would steal away to rest. In following the example of my Savior Jesus Christ, I would also like to find times to rest. God, I am pleading for the ability to rest peacefully. Cradle me in Your care and clear my head and thoughts. I know I am Your own, and I believe peace and rest are possible in You. Thank You in advance for real rest in my mind, spirit, and body. In the name of Jesus I pray, amen.

## SCRIPTURAL FOCUS

### Psalms 4:8

"I will both lie down in peace, and sleep; for You alone, O Lord, make me dwell in safety."

**Matthew 11:28-29**

"Come to Me, all you who labor and are heavy laden, and I will give you rest. Take My yoke upon you and learn from Me, for I am gentle and lowly in heart, and you will find rest for your souls."

## SINCERITY NOTES

You simply cannot handle all your loads, and everyone else's loads all the time. We were never meant to carry burdens alone. You have a Savior who also felt pain and took time to rest. Truly resting is not just a physical state—it is also mental and spiritual. Give it to the Lord and rest in His care.

I do not rest because

_____

_____

_____

_____

Is your sleep interrupted? _____

Have you tried praying about it or praying yourself to sleep?

_____

_____

_____

_____

Have you tried practical things like going to bed at a certain time, sleeping without a TV or radio, exercise, not eating after a certain time, playing water sounds on low, etc.? When? Were you consistent?

_____

_____

_____

_____

# Day _____

# Healing for a Loved One

Father, I come to you right now saying, "thank You." Thank You for the times when I am well. Thank You for the times when I am not so well, but still have the strength to press forward. Father, I say, "thank You," because Your Word tells me that in all things, we should give thanks. So, "Thank you, God."

Father, my loved one is sick, and I am asking you to cover them. Cover them with the power of Your blood. Father, seal it in Your love, so it can forever be sealed. Father, I am asking that You take away the pain _____ is feeling. Take away any lack that will come attached to the pain in the body and the aching in the mind and in the heart.

Father, I ask that You replenish everything poured out through sickness. God, everything that has come to attack, rob, and annihilate the joy that comes with good health, demolish it in the most spiritual realms. I am seeking You, Lord, and praying for a bountiful amount of wealth and healing into the life of _____. I am praying multitudes of healing power through the blood of Jesus Christ who was slain to save us from all sins. Father, Your Word declares that by your stripes we are healed. So, I am asking God that the healing power of the blood that flowed from my Savior on Calvary's cross begins to flow throughout the body of _____.

God penetrate their very soul and spirit with healing power. Father, reach out to places we cannot touch. I know I cannot heal, but I can ask You in prayer, oh Great Physician, and You will heal. You are mighty, You are powerful, and You are able, dear Father, to bring forth a fulfilled result. God, please do a great work in _____ because they have labored for You.

God, they have suffered for You. They have lived their life before You in a manner worthy of Your precious healing. Consider them worthy of another chance, worthy of the benefits, and worthy of the promises laid out throughout Your Word. Father, I know healing is our portion, because You are a God who loves us. You are a God who protects us. You are a God who stands by us. Father, heal right now in the name of Jesus like only You can. Father, if it is an unclean spirit, detach it. If it is unforgiveness, bring it to _____'s mind so they can forgive and let it go. God, please give _____ the strength to be able to forgive or even apologize if that is Your will. Father, if anything seen or unseen has attached to _____ that is unlike You, please remove it so healing may not be blocked.

Father, please send Your healing power forth like a never-ending well. I trust you to do these things because when I call upon You, the one true living Savior, You will answer. So, I am asking You to do it right now, God. Expand health, expand wealth, and multiply Your powerful breath throughout the body of _____. Expand the prosperity of healing, Father. The wealth and fullness of Your healing power is unimaginable. Lord, do the unthinkable and amaze our minds with Your power.

Thank you, God, in advance for all You will do. I thank You for the turnaround in _____'s body, God. I thank You for the turnaround in their mind. I even thank You for the turnaround in their spirit. Father, do it in the healing name of Jesus, like only You can. It is in the healing name of Jesus I pray, amen.

## SCRIPTURAL FOCUS

### Isaiah 53:5

"But He was wounded for our transgressions, He was bruised for our iniquities; the chastisement for our peace was upon Him, and by His stripes we are healed."

### James 5:14-15

"Is anyone among you sick? Let him call for the elders of the church, and let them pray over him, anointing him with oil in the name of the Lord. And the prayer of faith will save the sick, and the Lord will raise him up. And if he has committed sins, he will be forgiven."

## SINCERITY NOTES

I know God is a healer because

_____

_____

_____

_____

Find an example in the Bible where the Lord healed someone.

_____

_____

_____

How can the example you used help with your faith of being healed?

_____

_____

_____

_____

Remind yourself healing comes on Earth and in heaven. However it comes, healing is still your portion.

# Day _____

# Healing for Yourself

G od, I come to you today knowing illness has corrupted my body. I have known You to be a healer before, and I believe You will do the same thing again. No matter what I face, no matter what I am up against, I know You are always right there with me. You are the God who will never leave me nor forsake me. When I went through _____ before, You were the God who was with me. You are with me even now as I deal with _____.

Now Lord, I'm asking You to show yourself strong and do even more than You did before. God help me walk through this as a testimony to others who need to see and hear my story to see You. Help me get past this. Help me be strong enough to be mindful that You are able to be the cure. Father, You are the God who transcends generations. Jesus, You are the Savior whose blood exceeds any sickness or disease. God, You are the God of all who can heal all and who can restore all. God, I am asking You to call my body under subjection and help it operate in the manner in which it was created. Father, please help me walk forward in freedom from sickness and disease and to walk onward in a way uncommon to man. Please make my healing so powerful it will surprise my doctors and everyone around me.

Father, I stand in anticipation of being a walking testimony, a living and breathing miracle, and an overcomer by the blood of Jesus Christ that has unlimited power. I thank you in advance for my healing and I lift up a worship right now. God, I believe it is already done, and it is so good to know You are able to heal me. I don't think it. I don't imagine it. I know it, because I trust in You, and I trust You will do it for me. I understand You love me, God, because You sent Your Son as a sacrifice to save me.

God, I appreciate You, I thank You, and I am agreeing with the Holy Spirit that I will be healed. In Jesus's mighty name, I declare healing all over my life! And I believe no generational curse, no stronghold, no bondage, and nothing that has attached itself to me will be victorious! I will be victorious as a testament of Your healing power! It is so, by the blood of the Lamb who was slain! Thank You Jesus for Your blood. Thank You for Your power, God! in the name of Jesus I pray and believe, amen.

## SCRIPTURAL FOCUS

### 2 Kings 20:5

"Return and tell Hezekiah the leader of My people, 'Thus says the Lord, the God of David your father: "I have heard your prayer, I have seen your tears; surely I will heal you." On the third day you shall go up to the house of the Lord.'"

### Psalms 6:2

"Have mercy on me, O Lord, for I am weak; O Lord, heal me, for my bones are troubled."

### Jeremiah 17:14

"Heal me, O Lord, and I shall be healed; save me, and I shall be saved, for You are my praise."

**1 Peter 2:24**

"Who Himself bore our sins in His own body on the tree, that we, having died to sins, might live for righteousness—by whose stripes you were healed."

## SINCERITY NOTES

The enemy will try to derail you from accomplishing what God has for you to do. If he cannot influence you to give up on your own, then he will try other tactics. Often, when he cannot shake your faith, he will attack your health. He will attack something you cannot control in an attempt to control you. The enemy doesn't want your possessions. He wants you to give up on God. If he can keep you focused on pity, a lack of faith in your healing, and depression, instead of prayer and praise, then he can keep you from your breakthrough. Battling sickness and dealing with life's struggles can really deplete you physically and mentally, but your Father is a healer!

Father, please heal me in the area of

_____

_____

_____

_____

I know God is a healer because

_____

_____

_____

_____

You can reach out to others for your healing; but when you pray for yourself, something else breaks in the spirit. You need to stand boldly in the strength and authority the Lord has given you. Pray healing over yourself and do not move from it.

My personal prayer of healing is:

_____

_____

_____

_____

# Day _____

# Prayers for the World

L ord, I thank You for the Earth You have placed me on. I thank You for the World that surrounds me. I thank You for the family You provided. I thank You for the friends and the connections You've given to me in this world. Father, I even thank You for the good and the bad I have experienced while living in this world. It has not always been an easy life, but I grow more each day with every experience.

Father, help me know while I am living here that I have a duty to draw others to You. God, sometimes in that drawing, it gets hard. It also gets complicated, Lord. We live in a world where some people have itching ears and reject the existence of Jesus Christ. Help me remain diligent in spreading Your love and helping others to know You in a real and personal way.

Although bad things happen, it does not supersede the good You are doing. For I know Your Word is true when it says all things work together for the good of them who love God and are called according to His purpose. Father, I thank You for Your purpose, and I thank You for all You have done.

Lord, there are wars and rumors of wars, and things we have heard in the past are now coming to pass. Thank You that even in the midst of sicknesses, diseases, and trials, You are still the healer, the cure, and the righteous judge. Even when struggles are evident, I thank You for being

Emmanuel—God with us. Thank You for being near us all. I thank You for being a God who is with us, no matter what we are facing.

Father, even watching the news has become more than simply informational. It can be depressing for some. I ask that You help us be well-informed without being overtaken by the detriment and the sorrow that can be presented. Help us not to become jaded to the pain and turmoil often presented. I pray more upbeat, intentional, and positive messages are also shared through media outlets. Help us know You are a God who is still working, and that there are still good people left on this Earth.

Help us understand You are coming back, and we need to be ready. Forgive us, Lord, where we have fallen short and help us uplift our fellow man. Free us from a negative self-mentality and cause us to look at the kingdom as one body of Christ with many moving parts. Implore us to embrace You as our only Savior and give us the strength to stand by that truth. In a world where so many options are before us, help us to know You alone are the only real option.

Father, I ask You to help us remember that no enemy on Earth can defeat us. Nor can any enemy in the spiritual realm defeat us, because we are Your very own, and You are our God. We are victorious through You, Father! We know that in the end of all of this, we win! We are working toward our prize in heaven. We are working toward our goal of being with You forevermore.

I love You, I honor You, and I trust You. Thank You, Lord, that while I am here, I will be strong enough, able enough, capable enough, and present enough to do my part and tell people about my Lord and Savior, Jesus Christ. You are the one who can save us all from our sins. Father, I also want to push the message of love to let people know You love them without hesitation. Your love covers a multitude of sins. Your love can save us. I thank You for Your love. It is in Jesus' mighty name I pray, amen.

## SCRIPTURAL FOCUS

### 2 Chronicles 7:14

"If My people who are called by My name will humble themselves, and pray and seek My face, and turn from their wicked ways, then I will hear from heaven, and will forgive their sin and heal their land."

### Psalms 121:1-2

"I will lift up my eyes to the hills. From whence comes my help? My help comes from the Lord, who made heaven and earth."

### John 3:16

"For God so loved the world that He gave His only begotten Son, that whoever believes in Him should not perish but have everlasting life."

## SINCERITY NOTES

The world around us can be unsettling. The news can be informational and disheartening. No matter how much the world can cause you to think the enemy is in control, know that is not the case. Good still outweighs evil, and in the end, the kingdom of God will remain. Do not stress about what is going on all around you. Silence the outside noise so you can listen to what is going on within you. Pray for the world as the Holy Spirit leads you to pray. Trust that your prayers will make a difference. You have the power to help shift the world.

Lord, today I pray for the world because

_____

_____

_____

_____

# Day _____

# Warfare

G od, I know as long as I live in this world, good and evil will exist. I know there is a heaven, and I know there is a hell. I know there is a Father (God), Son (Jesus), and Holy Spirit (Holy Ghost), and I know there is a devil and his advocates Father, please help me as I suit up for battle daily. Help me put on the full armor of God. Help me pick up the Bible, the sword of truth, and wield it as a mighty weapon.

God, help me realize when I go to fight, it is not with my words, nor is it with my fist—but it is with power You have given me. It is with the authority You have bestowed upon me. Father, I ask that You help me not to be timid, and not to react out of the flesh, but in the spirit. Father, I seek You right now to strengthen me. Please teach my hands to war. Teach my mind to fight. God, teach me to dig into the most spiritual places for strength to fight back against the enemy. I recognize I am the head and not the tail. I know I am above and not beneath. I am victorious through You. There is nothing I can do on my own, but I can do all things through Christ who strengthens me.

Father, no matter what enemy comes against me, he cannot overpower me. No matter what attacks come for me, they cannot be victorious over me. For, as long as I serve You, I am serving the right Master, and victory is assured. I serve the one true and living God. I serve the Savior of my life and of the world. I serve a God who cannot be defeated. I ask You to help me walk daily in the knowledge of knowing defeat is not a possibility. In this world I will have tribulation, but I don't have to worry, because you have already overcome the world.

God, thank You for being with me and thank You for never leaving me. I appreciate You for times when I am not feeling strong, and You give me the energy to fight on. God, help me move forward as a mighty warrior for Your kingdom and protect me when I am on the battlefield. Protect me when I am standing in battle for my family, my friends, and even for myself. Father, help me when my body is attacked. Help me when my mind is attacked. Help me when people around me I love are being attacked. I believe there is victory in You, and I believe in the power and authority I carry through the blood of Jesus Christ who was slain. Help me, Father, to tap into that power and not lose sight of it.

Help me walk into war and have the ability to shift the very foundations of hell! Aid me in being able to speak a thing and heaven sends a response because I am Your child. Help me to know there is work You would have me do. There is a war that has been waged, and I thank You, God, that I am on the right side of the battle. I am surely with the winning team! Father, be with me, teach me, and grow me up spiritually. Continue to help me be prepared for every battle. Lord, I love You, and I thank You. It is in the mighty name of Jesus I pray, amen.

## SCRIPTURAL FOCUS

### Ephesians 6:10-18

"Finally, my brethren, be strong in the Lord and in the power of His might. Put on the whole armor of God, that you may be able to stand against the wiles of the devil. For we do not wrestle against flesh and blood, but against principalities, against powers, against the rulers of the darkness of this age, against spiritual hosts of wickedness in the heavenly places. Therefore take up the whole armor of God, that you may be able to withstand in the evil day, and having done all, to stand. Stand therefore, having girded your waist with truth, having put on the breastplate of righteousness, and having shod your feet with the preparation of the gospel of peace; above all, taking the shield of faith with which you will be able to quench all the fiery darts of the wicked one. And take the helmet of salvation, and the sword of the Spirit, which is the word of God; praying always with all prayer and supplication in the Spirit, being watchful to this end with all perseverance and supplication for all the saints."

## 1 Peter 5:8-9

"Be sober, be vigilant; because your adversary the devil walks about like a roaring lion, seeking whom he may devour. Resist him, steadfast in the faith, knowing that the same sufferings are experienced by your brotherhood in the world."

## Deuteronomy 31:6

"Be strong and of good courage, do not fear nor be afraid of them; for the Lord your God, He is the One who goes with you. He will not leave you nor forsake you."

## SINCERITY NOTES

If the enemy is causing you great pain right now, locate your weapons of warfare. You have to fight! While in battle, you are gaining strength, wisdom, perseverance, and staying power. You WILL come out of this. You WILL live. You WILL prosper. You WILL win! In Jesus' mighty name.

Are you in pain right now? Why?

_____

_____

_____

What can you do to combat the attacks of the enemy?

# Day _____

# Chain-breaking Prayer

Lord, I come to You now on behalf of myself and my family. I have become aware of similarities and consistencies throughout my bloodline that I do not want to plague my life. I am asking You to allow me to be the chain breaker in my family. The attacks on my lineage have to cease.

I pray against every attack that has come against me and my family from conception to take us out. I pray against plaguing, monitoring and familiar spirits that would come to keep us stagnant and keep any of us from walking forward into our destiny. I ask You, God, to stretch forth Your hand and reach back through my generations to the root of the issue. Uproot what holds hollow souls empty and fill the voids with Your love and tender mercies. Lord, I ask that You pluck out the very core of the stronghold and render the spirit attached to it powerless in the name of Jesus!

Father, I'm asking You to mute every tongue. Expose every plot and scheme of the enemy and his camp! Devour every devious incantation, spell, hex, root, or demonic tie that has tried to bind us. Take power away from every diabolical attachment that has been assigned to my family. Lord, I ask You to rise up and fall mighty through the power of Your blood and flow over unclean blood ties, allegiances, oaths, curses, plots, strongholds, and ties that hold generations of families captive by the evil one. I am a chain breaker, and the curses and strongholds on my family tree stop with me! I shall not fall victim or pray to any form of bondage that has tormented other family members in the past. I believe cords are severed, singed, and unhinged by the double-edged sword of Your Word and the blood of the Lamb! I am asking You to cast every foul thing back to the pits of hell from whence it came and where it belongs.

Father, I stand up now denouncing anything I allowed into my life and ask You to severe attachments to anything tainted in my lineage that has led to me. I will not be a victim of my circumstances and will be an overcomer! I refuse to be a host for the works of the enemy when I have freedom through You! I am the chain breaker! I am delivered, and I am set free, in the name of Jesus and by the power of His blood—the blood that still has power! For it is in the mighty, healing name of Jesus I ask all these things and pray, amen and amen.

## SCRIPTURAL FOCUS

### Psalms 27:1-2

"The Lord is my light and my salvation; Whom shall I fear? The Lord is the strength of my life; of whom shall I be afraid? When the wicked came against me to eat up my flesh, my enemies and foes, they stumbled and fell."

### 2 Corinthians 5:17

"Therefore, if anyone is in Christ, he is a new creation; old things have passed away; behold, all things have become new."

### Ephesians 6:12

"For we do not wrestle against flesh and blood, but against principalities, against powers, against the rulers of the darkness of this age, against spiritual hosts of wickedness in the heavenly places."

# SINCERITY NOTES

*"A generational stronghold is a defilement, abuse or mindset affecting the soul that is passed down from one generation to another."*

SJJ

What signs of generational strongholds do you see in your family?

_____

_____

_____

_____

Do any of them exist with you? Which ones?

_____

_____

_____

_____

If you need the Lord to free you, just ask Him. You are the one who breaks the chain! Believe it and do the work to be free. What steps will you take to be free?

_____

_____

_____

# Day _____

# Fasting

Father, I come to You now saying, "Thank You." Thank you for all You have done for me. Thank You for all You will do, Lord. I want to be strengthened in Your Word, and I desire to be strengthened in my prayer life. Lord, I know I also need to pair the two of those with fasting. For Your Word tells me some things only leave through fasting and prayer. So, Lord, teach me how to dig deeper into my prayer life and how to fast. I want to be able to fast to deny myself and to open myself to You. Father, please empty me of everything that is not worthy and fill me with everything that is earnest and right.

Please help me not to only turn down my plate, but to turn down any indignation, any unrighteousness, and anything that is unlike you, Lord. Take away every hardness of my heart. Take away every version of unforgiveness I may be harboring, Father. Bring everything to my mind that I need to go and get right so I can go before You in this fast and be ready. I am totally open to receive, Father. I know fasting is a period when I can hear from You, and I know there will be temptations all around me. Father, you know the things I am tempted by. You know what the enemy will put before me. So, I am asking in advance that You give me the strength to make it through and to hold on. Lord, Your Word tells me there is no temptation that has overtaken me that You have not already provided a way of escape to resist. So, thank You, God, for that way out.

Right now, in the name of Jesus, I pray each time I fast that I get stronger, and I grow deeper. As I go deeper, teach me things in the spiritual realms and open pathways to prepare me for what I need to know in the spirit. Father, please show me beyond this earthly realm and outfit me with keen spiritual insight. Show me what You would have me see. Father, direct my mind toward the things of the Spirit, so I may be prepared to fight spiritually. During this time of fasting, strengthen my armor, Lord. Please help me put on the full armor of God so I can stand against the wiles of the devil.

Help me, Father, to be a vessel for You. Put the people on my heart who You would have me pray for doing this time. Lord, I thank You, I trust You, and I am believing You that when I come out of this fast, I will be stronger than when I started. I have faith I will be more powerful, and I will have the tools You have given me to fight even further. I thank You, God, for success in this fast—not as man sees it, but as You see it. Thank You, Lord, for seeing me through this accomplishment of obedience and sacrifice. It is in the mighty name of Jesus I pray, amen.

## SCRIPTURAL FOCUS

### Ezra 8:23

"So we fasted and entreated our God for this, and He answered our prayer."

### Psalm 19:14

"Let the words of my mouth and the meditation of my heart be acceptable in Your sight, o Lord, my strength and my Redeemer."

### Matthew 17:20-21

"So Jesus said to them, 'Because of your unbelief; for assuredly, I say to you, if you have faith as a mustard seed, you will say to this mountain, "Move from here to there," and it will move; and nothing will be impossible for you. However, this kind does not go out except by prayer and fasting.'"

## SINCERITY NOTES

*Fasting is a disciplined act of obedience that denies the flesh and strengthens the spirit.*

SJJ

Fasting is not just a good thing to do for the New Year. If we want to shed the old self and put on a new level of maturity, fasting is required. Fasting is not only about denying yourself, but it is about finding yourself in Him.

Do you desire to grow and be strengthened through fasting? _____

Ask the Lord what type of fast you should do. Fasting does not only involve food—it can include the exclusion of activities, habits, things we enjoy, etc. It will also often involve the inclusion of reading the Bible, praying, worshipping, etc. It can also be for a variety of time frames. The purpose of the fast is also very important. It will provide your end goal and your prayer focus. Pray and take one step at a time. What has the Lord told you in prayer?

Type of fast? _____

What to exclude?

_____

_____

_____

_____

What to include?

_____

_____

_____

_____

Length of the fast? _____

Purpose of the fast?

_____

_____

_____

_____

After you finish your fast, write down the results. What did you learn, hear and gain from the fast?

_____

_____

_____

_____

# Day _____

# Direction

*Even if you do not know what God is doing through you, do what He says. In obedience to Him, He will reveal His purpose to you.*

SJJ

Father, I am grateful for You, and I thank You for this day. I am seeking You today for direction. Your Word tells me the steps of a righteous man are ordered, so I am asking that You see me through the eyes of Your righteousness. Father, make me worthy through Your power. Give me clarity on what You would have me do next. It seems like certain aspects of my life are at a standstill right now, and I do not know what to do. I do not know which path to take, and honestly, Lord, I really do not see what You would have me do next. Please, Father, I am asking You to speak to me and show me which way to go. Show me what You will for my life, and I will respond. God, until You show me the move to make, teach me how to wait in the interim.

When I read through Your Word, many people with great purpose had to wait. Father, when you sent the Prophet Samuel to seek out David to tell him he would be king, David had to wait. His word was not for that moment, but it was for a later appointed time. Father, I know people have spoken into my life. I know there are even things I sense in my spirit about me—things I believe will come to pass and things You have told me in prayer. Father, until they happen, teach me how to wait. Show me how to pause and pray. Show me what You would have me do in the waiting times.

Lord, help me to be a vessel for right now. Help me serve You eagerly and wisely in these days. I pray nothing I do hinders me from the vision You have for my life. Help my vision to line up with Your will. Help me seek out Your will for my life and not that of my own. I desire to be in Your will. I want to be in tune with Your words and Your way for me, and not with my flesh. There are things I desire, but if they are not what You desire for me, please take the longing for them away from me. Show me what You want so I can understand what I need to focus on and what my direction and purpose are in life.

Father, I honor you because I believe You are working it out for my good. I trust the principle of Romans 8:28. *"And we know that all things work together for good to those who love God, to those who are the called according to His purpose."* I believe it is already happening. I believe You are calling me to do great things. I am asking, Father, that You lay them before me and guide me through every step. If the step is "go," then help me move. If the step is "wait," then help me stand still. Teach me and help me to pray and fast and to remain engulfed in Your Word through it all.

God, I thank You. I want to be efficient for You and effective for Your Kingdom. Help me not only to be busy, but to be effective. I honor You, Lord, and I believe and trust that everything I have asked You will do—and even more. It is in Jesus' mighty name I pray, amen.

## SCRIPTURAL FOCUS

### Psalm 119:133

"Direct my steps by Your word, and let no iniquity have dominion over me."

**Proverbs 3:5-6**

"Trust in the Lord with all your heart and lean not on your own understanding; in all your ways acknowledge Him, and He shall direct your paths."

**Jeremiah 33:3**

"Call to Me, and I will answer you, and show you great and mighty things, which you do not know."

## SINCERITY NOTES

I give myself a reminder daily by saying, "I'm exactly where God wants me to be right now." You too are exactly where God wants you to be right now. I believe today will be your day. I believe a breakthrough waits around the corner with your name on it. A blessing hides in the midst of the turmoil that may surround you. I trust and pray a whisper from God's voice today reaches only your ears. When you strain to hear that whisper, allow it to resonate loudly in your spirit. Keep being unrelenting about pressing into Him for your joy. He will respond.

# Day _____

# God, I Need You

Lord, I thank You for this day. I show gratitude for You being with me. I thank You for being my all in all. I know You, but God, I need You right now. I need You in a way I do not think I have asked You to be there for me in a long time. Father, I need You to be my strength. I need You to be my guiding light. God, be the force that moves me forward—because today, I cannot do it on my own. I am giving it over to You, because Your Word tells me to cast my cares upon You because You care for me. So, I am giving You everything, God, because I have been holding on long enough.

I do not know how this situation will work out. Although I do not know how things will turn out, I know I trust You. I trust You with my all, God. I trust You with every fiber of my being. I believe in Your Word when it tells me You will not leave me nor forsake me. God, work it out for Your glory—not because I am asking, but because I know You are able. Thank You in advance for Your provision. I worship You in advance for Your sustaining power. I praise You in advance for victory on the other side of this storm. I recognize You as my peace in the midst of it all. I honor You, I trust You, and I believe in You. In the name of Jesus I pray, amen.

## SCRIPTURAL FOCUS

### Psalm 39:12

"Hear my prayer, O Lord, and give ear to my cry; Do not be silent at my tears; for I am a stranger with You, A sojourner, as all my fathers were."

**Romans 8:26**

"Likewise the Spirit also helps in our weaknesses. For we do not know what we should pray for as we ought, but the Spirit Himself makes intercession for us with groanings which cannot be uttered."

**2 Corinthians 4:8-9**

"We are hard-pressed on every side, yet not crushed; we are perplexed, but not in despair; persecuted, but not forsaken; struck down, but not destroyed."

**1 Peter 5:7**

"Casting all your care upon Him, for He cares for you."

## SINCERITY NOTES

My years have been filled with things that broke down my mind, my body, and my heart. Some of it was my doing, and some of it was fallout from my ancestors' decisions. It is good to know the Lord holds my spirit—unbroken, unwavering, and full of faith. Trust He will do the same for you. No matter what you have endured in life, know that **being broken is beneficial.** God knows what you are going through and have been through, and He is merging the pieces together to make you complete and whole.

Give your cares to the Lord and He will see you through this situation. Do you believe that He will?

_____

_____

_____

_____

If so, why?

_____

_____

_____

_____

If not, why not?

_____

_____

_____

_____

What steps can you take daily to trust in God more?

_____

_____

_____

_____

# Day _____

# Peace and Protection

God, I come to You thanking You for this day I have never seen before. I thank You for another opportunity to serve You. Thank You for everything You have done for me thus far. Father, today I need to understand Your peace. I need to feel Your peace around me. It seems like I am hearing things on the news that make it seem as if your children are outnumbered. God, help me not to pay attention to what is coming through the airwaves, but to pay attention to the Word You have hidden in my heart. Help me pay attention to Your Word where it says, "When the enemy comes in like a flood The Spirit of the Lord will lift up a standard against him" (Isaiah 59:19 KJV).

Help me remember I can have peace that surpasses all understanding. God, the same way You told the winds and the waves "Peace, be still" (Mark 4:39 KJV), speak to my spirit and tell it "Peace, be still." God, please help me. Sometimes I do not know which way to go. Sometimes I do not know which direction to take, but I know at every turn, You are there. God help me rest in Your peace today. I really need You, and I thank You for being with me.

God, I also ask that You give peace to those connected to me and those around me in various arenas of life. Father, even give peace to people who may not consider me a good person. Lord, when it comes to people who may not see You within me, illuminate their eyes and give them peace. Help our spirits to resonate with each other. Help us connect through the knowledge of and belief in You. Help me to have peace in all things. Help me to know You are there. Help me to understand You will always protect me. You will shield me as a mighty strong fortress. God, I thank You for being my strong tower. I thank You for the fortified walls of prayer. I thank You, Father, for always keeping me calm when I need You most.

God, thank You for Your peace that is overcoming me right now. I allow You in even more. I believe Your love is enveloping me like a warm spiritual blanket. God, I thank You right now for being with me. Thank You for protecting me. I thank You for Your peace that surpasses all understanding. I do not know how you do it, God, but I know You have done it in me, and I praise You right now. I praise You, Father, for Your peace and protection. And I believe You so I can become stronger and more at peace each day. It is in the calming name of Jesus I pray, amen.

## SCRIPTURAL FOCUS

### Isaiah 26:3

"You will keep him in perfect peace, whose mind is stayed on You, because he trusts in You."

### Isaiah 59:19

"When the enemy comes in like a flood, the Spirit of the Lord will lift up a standard against him."

**John 16:33** "These things I have spoken to you, that in Me you may have peace. In the world you will have tribulation; but be of good cheer, I have overcome the world."

**2 Thessalonians 3:16**

"Now may the Lord of peace Himself give you peace always in every way. The Lord be with you all."

## SINCERITY NOTES

Peace is a state of mind as well as a state of being. The one true and living God can carry you through a storm while giving you total peace. Storms always blow over in due time. May the Lord cover every part of your being that needs peace during this season. May the peace of God penetrate your mind and pierce your heart with comforting love. I pray for a supernatural calmness over your entire being. In the mighty name of Jesus, amen.

Write down some steps you can take to limit stressors and gain more peace.

_____

_____

_____

_____

# Day _____

# Miracles

*He's more than able! God still works miracles. We just miss*
*them while trying to create our own signs and wonders.*

SJJ

Father, I come to You right now saying, "Thank you." God, I thank You for the ability to seek You in prayer. I honor You for Your love that surrounds me. I even thank You that in the midst of what I am dealing with, You are there. Father, You know what I am facing. You know what my family is facing. God, I am seeking You right now for a miracle. I know You are a miracle worker. You did miracles all throughout Your Word. I have read about it. I have heard about it. I have seen it, God. I need one of those miracles right now. In the name of Jesus, I need You to show yourself strong. Not because You have to, but because I know You are able to.

_____ needs a miracle. He/ She needs You to come through like never before. So, I am asking You to be the miraculous God You are! I know You can show up for whatever is needed in this moment. Please offer healing to their body, soul, spirit, and mind. God, please do the same for me so I can stay in a place of being ready to fight on behalf of my loved ones. Guide me so I can be in a place where I understand You still heal, and You still deliver.

Lord, I am praying for my family members that are plagued in their minds. I am asking You to give them a miraculous healing. Please remember my family, remember my friends and Your children everywhere who are dealing with broken finances and poverty. I ask that You help them with the spirit that is perplexing them, God. I ask that You teach them the principles of tithing and sowing. Teach them the principles of giving first fruits to You. God, I believe that in exchange You are going to give healing and deliverance, and You are going to make our crooked paths prosperous. I thank You, Father, for setting us on the right path.

Thank You that You are still a miracle worker and a promise keeper. Father, I am asking You right now to show miracles, signs, and wonders. I am asking You to be the God of the Old Testament and Savior of New Testament—the One who is, who was, and who is to come. Please be the God who is the epitome of a miracle. Jesus, I thank You for what You have done through living Your life in the form of human flesh—being all human and all God at the same time. Thank You for being crucified on our behalf and taking on our sins, being buried, and being resurrected from the dead. God, that is the ultimate miracle! It is an unimaginable miracle, but one we know to be true in our hearts.

Thank You for being the miraculous God. I am asking that You do miracles over and over and over again. I stand in anticipation of the praise reports that will break forth in the coming days, and I position myself ready for praises to Your holy name. You are almighty God, and no one compares to You. Please help me not to deviate from Your will. When the enemy comes in to try to trick me and attack my faith, remind me of these words—He can work it out! I trust You, and I believe You are going to show Yourself strong. Lord, I believe it is already done! I will not move from the fact that it is already done! It is so, and it shall not be otherwise! In the miracle-working name of Jesus I pray, amen.

## SCRIPTURAL FOCUS

### Psalm 77:14

"You are the God who does wonders; You have declared Your strength among the peoples."

### Luke 18:27

"But He said, 'The things which are impossible with men are possible with God.'"

## SINCERITY NOTES

Things don't always work out the way you planned, but God's plan always prevails. Keep your thoughts directed toward Him. Remember you cannot always see a miracle in the natural because we serve a Supernatural God. When God is in the midst, miracles manifest. May the atmosphere shift in your favor. There is still a blessing tailor-made just for you. It is on the way.

Make a list of people you know in need of a miracle and intentionally pray over them. Your prayers have power.

_____

_____

_____

_____

How were their prayers answered?

_____

_____

_____

_____

# Day _____

# God is With Me

Father, I come thanking You right now. You have been so good to me, and You are such a blessing in my life. I do not know how I could ever make it without You. When I think about Your goodness, it is overwhelming.

When I consider everything You saved me from, it blesses my soul. I know there are so many things You have protected me from that I did not even see. I know there were so many attacks on my life, and You just stretched out Your hands, blocked them, and said, "No!" I thank You for the things I can see and especially for the things You shielded me from viewing. Lord, I thank You for being my ever-present help.

I enjoy having a relationship with You. I know You are with me, because I can sense Your presence, and I can feel Your love surrounding me. When I am having a bad day, I can bow my head and say, "Jesus," and instantly, You are near. I feel You with every fiber of my being.

Lord, even when I try to explain to others what You mean to me, profound words escape me. I can tell them about Jesus' sacrifice and how He died and rose to save us from our sins. I can tell them about all the promises found throughout Your Word. I can tell them about how You healed me and how You delivered me. I can share about how I have seen You set the captives free and how You delivered people from unclean spirits. But Lord, when I try to dig deep and express the magnitude of how You are there for me, the words are far from me. Everything You are to me is indescribable.

As I pray this prayer, Lord, I feel the tears welling up. I am overwhelmed and overcome with the magnitude of Your love. You are truly amazing! You are the epitome of awesome! I do not even know why we take the time to call other things AMAZING and AWESOME and WONDERFUL, because You, Lord, are the only one who can justify the use of those words. You are my God. You are my Savior, and I know You are with me. I know You will not leave me. I know with all truth that nothing can separate me from Your love—not death, not life, not people, not height nor depth, not angels, and surely not principalities nor powers, not anything! God, You are with me when I am sick, when people forsake me, when people leave me, and when I lose things. Even on the days when I feel alone, none of that is real, because You are with me. You are my ever-present and constant help, and I love You. I adore You, and I will do this forever more. It is in Jesus' name I pray, amen.

## SCRIPTURAL FOCUS

### Romans 8:38-39

"For I am persuaded that neither death nor life, nor angels nor principalities nor powers, nor things present nor things to come, nor height nor depth, nor any other created thing, shall be able to separate us from the love of God which is in Christ Jesus our Lord."

### 1 Corinthians 3:16

"Do you not know that you are the temple of God and that the Spirit of God dwells in you?"

## SINCERITY NOTES

The Holy Spirit working inside of you will testify to others that you serve a God who is bigger than you. Do not worry about if you will say the right thing or always get "it" right. Just know when you're a child of the King, He works on your behalf. Thank you, Lord, for being who You are. I trust You!

Do you feel the Lord is with you? _____

Why or why not?

_____

_____

_____

_____

What are some steps you can take to strengthen your relationship with the to be more secure in His presence?

_____

_____

_____

_____

# Day _____

# Greatness in Him

Lord, please help me tap into my greatness. Let me understand attacks will come because I made a choice to serve You. It was the best choice I could have ever made. Even though it was an excellent choice, sometimes this walk can get hard, and I can feel defeated. Help me know that no matter how weak I think I am, I am strong through You. You are Jehovah Jireh, and you will provide for us as we stay rooted in Your will. Help us never believe the trick of the enemy, because we are not victims, but victors. We are great because You are great. We are a chosen generation. We are set apart for Your service, and we are more than conquerors through Christ Jesus. No plot will replace our productivity! No evil plan will throw us off course! I speak right direction and new dedication in the name of the Lion of Judah, Jesus Christ! It is so! Amen!

## SCRIPTURAL FOCUS

### Romans 8:37

"As it is written: 'For Your sake we are killed all day long; We are accounted as sheep for the slaughter.' Yet in all these things we are more than conquerors through Him who loved us."

### Philippians 4:13

"I can do all things through Christ who strengthens me."

## SINCERITY NOTES

I feel my weakest when

_____

_____

_____

_____

I feel my strongest when

_____

_____

_____

_____

I can be greater through God if I work on these things:

_____

_____

_____

_____

The only person who can cause you to fail is you. The enemy cannot do it because he does not have the authority to control you—he can only influence you. Are you living above his influence? _____

God can make you do anything, but He chose to give you free will. Your choices are your own. Choose life and greatness through Christ.

# Day _____

# Free Indeed

This day, I approach you, Lord, thanking You for the lives of those You have allowed to see another day. Thank You for releasing us from captivity over 2,000 years ago. Lord, today, I pray we all walk in that freedom by not being bound by the demonic chains sent to arrest our hearts and minds. I pray we understand that "freedom" is a state of being and not just a word we say nonchalantly. We are free! Our bands are loosed! We have power!

I speak true freedom over everyone who feels as if life and its circumstances have them in chains. I pray they take time to remember Your redemptive work on the cross and through Your resurrection. Help them know You are the gap filler who stood between them and the sting of death. I pray they shake off the false effects of the sting and understand the true freedom Your sacrifice provides. In the mighty and matchless name of Jesus I pray, amen.

## SCRIPTURAL FOCUS

### John 8:36

"Therefore if the Son makes you free, you shall be free indeed."

**Romans 5:8**

"But God demonstrates His own love toward us, in that while we were still sinners, Christ died for us."

**Romans 10:9**

"That if you confess with your mouth the Lord Jesus and believe in your heart that God has raised Him from the dead, you will be saved."

## SINCERITY NOTES

As long as we live this life, there will be days when we feel trapped or like there is no way out. Remind yourself that Christ has given you freedom through Him. If you are in need of reassurance, ask the Lord to give it to you. He hears you when you pray, and He wants you to be free in your heart, soul, and mind. Believe in Him, pray, and be free.

I am free in Christ because

_____

_____

_____

_____

# Bonus Day

# Home

Father, I thank You for the many blessings You have bestowed upon me. I thank You, Lord, for keeping me off the streets. I thank You for putting a roof over my head. Lord, before I ask anything for myself, I pray You touch those who are without a home. Father, touch those who are still seeking a new level in life. Touch those who do not have a covering and who may get affected by the elements. Father, I pray You give them a home and help them to stand. Aid them in getting the help they need to have opportunities to get off the streets. I pray resources find and assist them with a life change for the better.

Father, for saving me from that plight, I thank You. Lord, You blessed me with somewhere to live, and I am safe. Thank You for giving me comforts, and I praise Your holy name, because I know it could be another way. Lord, I am asking You to cover this home in Your Word. Seal it, Jesus, in Your blood. I ask You to keep us protected from pain, harm, fear, evil, and danger. Father, if anyone comes to the doorstep, and they are unlike You, I pray their spirit is so vexed they turn around and leave. Lord, if there is someone You would have to come in and sup with us, allow our spirits to agree, so we will know it is Your will.

Help us, Father, to be good stewards over what You have provided. Help us live the way You would have us to. Father, help us give back to You with time in prayer and time in doing Your will in this home. You have provided for us, Father. Help us seek out a space as our secret place to pray and talk with You. Lord, make it a place where we can go and meet You regularly so it is saturated with Your Spirit and Your love. I thank You for this home, and I praise Your holy name. I pray for every person who is praying for a home, and I ask You to bless them as You have blessed me, and even more. I appreciate all You have done, Lord, and I promise You this blessing is not wasted on me. Our home will be a place where You are honored. It is in Jesus' name I pray, amen.

## SCRIPTURAL FOCUS

### Joshua 24:15

"But as for me and my house, we will serve the Lord."

### Psalm 91:1-2

"He who dwells in the secret place of the Most High shall abide under the shadow of the Almighty. I will say of the Lord, 'He is my refuge and my fortress; My God, in Him I will trust.'"

### Psalm 127:1

"Unless the Lord builds the house, they labor in vain who build it; unless the Lord guards the city, The watchman stays awake in vain."

### Luke 10:5

"But whatever house you enter, first say, 'Peace to this house.'"

# SINCERITY NOTES

A home is a blessing from the Lord. Honor Him in it as He has provided for you. Seek Him in safety there and grow in your secret place.

List ways you can honor the Lord with your home.

_____

_____

_____

_____

# Personal Prayer

L ord, today, I come to You saying thank You for all You have done in
my life. Lord, today I am seeking You for

_____

_____

_____

_____

_____

_____

_____

_____

_____

_____

_____

In the name of Jesus I pray, amen.

## SCRIPTURAL FOCUS

### Psalms 5:3

"My voice You shall hear in the morning, O Lord; In the morning I will direct it to You, and I will look up."

## SINCERITY NOTES

_____

_____

_____

_____

_____

_____

_____

_____

# Prayer and

# Intercession List

We run into people in person, on the phone, or on social media. We often tell them we will pray for them, or we see them post a prayer request. It is easy to forget and move on with daily life. Use this list to track prayer requests. Do not forget to add your personal prayer pleas.


Person: _____

Prayer Request:

_____

_____

_____

_____


Person: _____

Prayer Request:

_____

_____

_____

_____

Person: _____

Prayer Request:

_____

_____

_____

_____

Person: _____

Prayer Request:

_____

_____

_____

_____

Person: _____

Prayer Request:

_____

_____

_____

_____


Person: _____

Prayer Request:

_____

_____

_____

_____


Person: _____

Prayer Request:

_____

_____

_____

_____


Person: _____

Prayer Request:

_____

_____

_____

_____


Person: _____

Prayer Request:

_____

_____

_____

_____


Person: _____

Prayer Request:

_____

_____

_____

_____


Person: _____

Prayer Request:

_____

_____

_____

_____


Person: _____

Prayer Request:

_____

_____

_____

_____


Person: _____

Prayer Request:

_____

_____

_____

_____


Person: _____

Prayer Request:

_____

_____

_____

_____

Person: _____

Prayer Request:

_____

_____

_____

_____

Person: _____

Prayer Request:

_____

_____

_____

_____

Person: _____

Prayer Request:

_____

_____

_____

_____


Person: _____

Prayer Request:

_____

_____

_____

_____

# Works Cited

Dictionary.com, LLC. 2024. https://www.dictionary.com/.

# About the Author

**Shirley J. Johnson** is an ordained Elder, servant leader, and overcomer. She has survived struggles with identity, sickness, tragic family loss, and the challenges of helping others while hurting.

She has spent more than 15 years leading ministries, teaching, and preaching at various engagements. Her love for God is the source of her strength. She has a genuine desire to serve God's people and does this through her non-profit organization, STILL JOYFUL MINISTRIES, where she imparts the truth that life and tragedy do not have to steal your joy. She helps individuals grow through their trials and remain joyful by standing on Nehemiah8:10, "**The joy of the Lord is your strength**."

Her background includes service in the U.S. Air Force and the Department of Homeland Security. She also has a degree in Communications from Dallas Baptist University. She is a Certified Christian Mentor (CCM), coauthor of *Lifting the Veil*, author of *From Comfort to Completion: Still Joyful*, and author of *Prayerful Plea: A 30-DayPrayer Devotional*. She has been featured in *Queen B Magazine*, *K.I.S.H. Magazine*, and *Voyage Dallas Magazine*.

For book signings or speaking engagements, you can reach Shirley J. Johnson by email at stilljoyfulministries@yahoo.com or visit her website at www.stilljoyfulministries.com. Follow her on Facebook and Instagram: @StillJoyfulMinistries

Made in the USA
Columbia, SC
29 January 2025

52505973R00076